Sports-Graphics

Every Second Counts

Kristy Stark

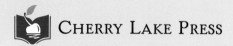

CHERRY LAKE PRESS

Published in the United States of America by Cherry Lake Publishing Group
Ann Arbor, Michigan
www.cherrylakepublishing.com

Reading Adviser: Beth Walker Gambro, MS, Ed., Reading Consultant, Yorkville, IL

Photo Credits: Cover: ©hvostik / Shutterstock; ©artisticco / Getty Images; ©stevezmina1 / Getty Images; ©msan10 / Getty Images; ©FARBAI / Getty Images; page 5: ©MisterEmil / Shutterstock; page 5: ©Anatolir / Shutterstock; page 5: ©Jessica Orozco / ; page 9: ©kupritz / Getty Images; page 11: ©Brian Babineau / Contributor / Getty Images; page 16: ©nikiteev_konstantin / Shutterstock; page 17: ©Ground Picture / Shutterstock; page 17: ©Jacob Lund / Shutterstock; page 19: ©Aşkın Dursun KAMBEROĞLU / Getty Images; page 19: ©rambo182 / Getty Images; page 19: ©Jessica Orozco / ; page 19: ©bounward / Getty Images; page 19: ©lushik / Getty Images; page 19: ©pop_jop / Getty Images; page 20: ©RUSSELLTATEdotCOM / Getty Images; page 22: ©molotovcoketail / Getty Images; page 23: ©GoodStudio / Shutterstock; page 26: ©Krafted / Shutterstock; page 27: ©biolalabet / Shutterstock

Cherry Lake Press is an imprint of Cherry Lake Publishing Group.

Library of Congress Cataloging-in-Publication Data
Library of Congress Cataloging-in-Publication Data has been filed and is available at catalog.loc.gov.

Cherry Lake Publishing Group would like to acknowledge the work of the Partnership for 21st Century Learning, a Network of Battelle for Kids. Please visit http://www.battelleforkids.org/networks/p21 for more information.

Printed in the United States of America

Note from publisher: Websites change regularly, and their future contents are outside of our control. Supervise children when conducting any recommended online searches for extended learning opportunities.

Kristy Stark writes books about a variety of topics, from sports to biographies to science topics. When she is not busy writing, she enjoys reading, camping, lounging at the beach, and doing just about anything outdoors. Most of all, she loves to spend time with her husband, daughter, son, and two lazy cats at their home in Southern California.

CONTENTS

A Matter of Seconds

The seconds on the clock tick down . . . 3 . . . 2 . . . 1. She shoots the ball. She scores just before the clock hits zero. The fans go wild!

No matter the sport, every second counts. So much can happen in a few seconds. The outcome of the game can even change in fractions of a second.

Every sport is timed. But the length of play time varies from sport to sport. Why are games, matches, and sprints timed? What can players do in a matter of seconds?

Units of Time

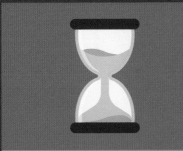

1 HOUR
has
60 MINUTES

1 MINUTE
has
60 SECONDS

1 SECOND
has
10 DECISECONDS

A Shot to Remember

Former Lakers guard Derek Fisher went down in history. It was the 2004 NBA playoffs. Fisher made a game winning shot. He released the ball with 0.4 seconds left on the game clock. The shot went in. His team won the game.

2020, NBA

CHAPTER 1

How Sports Are Timed

Every sport has its own way of dividing the game or match. Each part has a certain amount of time. A football game is divided into four quarters. In the National Football League (NFL), each quarter is 15 minutes. High school football games typically have 12-minute quarters.

Soccer is divided into halves. Each half is 45 minutes long for professional players. Younger players have much shorter halves.

Hockey games are played in three periods. Each period is 20 minutes long for the National Hockey League (NHL).

Quarters, Halves, and Periods in Sports

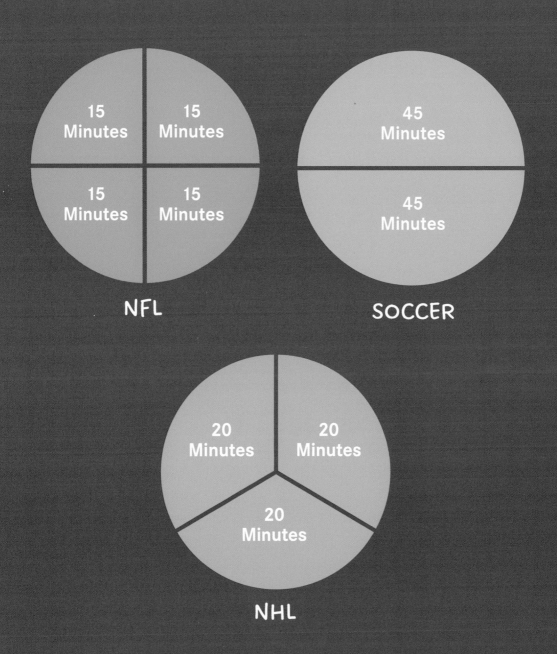

NFL
- 15 Minutes
- 15 Minutes
- 15 Minutes
- 15 Minutes

SOCCER
- 45 Minutes
- 45 Minutes

NHL
- 20 Minutes
- 20 Minutes
- 20 Minutes

2022, Rookie Road; 2022, FloHockey; 2022, Sports Illustrated

Stoppage Time

Professional soccer play time totals 90 minutes. But the matches often run longer than that.

- Referees stop the clock during the game. This happens for many reasons.
- Referees stop the game when a player is hurt. Play stops when a coach wants to make a player substitution, too.
- When the clock is stopped, the amount of stoppage time is noted. It is added to the end of the match.
- Average game clock stoppage is anywhere from 1 to 6 minutes. But it can be more than this.

game time **+** stoppage time 1-6 minutes **=** total time

2022, Rookie Road

World Cup Stoppage Time

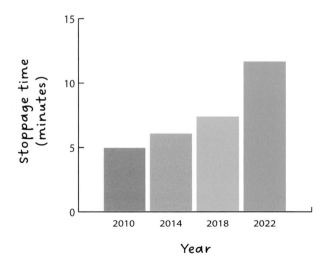

Year

The World Cup is one of the biggest sports events in the world. Each goal is celebrated for several minutes. This can lead to some lengthy stoppage time.

2023, Statista

Average NFL TV Broadcast

An NFL game clocks 60 minutes of playing time. The games last much longer. The length of the game depends on television coverage. Commercial breaks add time.

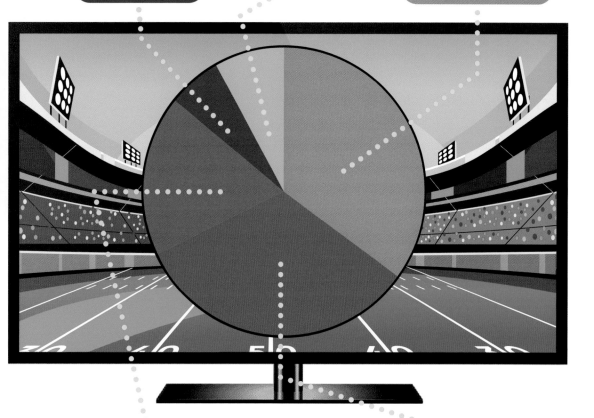

Replays
15 minutes

Game action
11 minutes

Shots of players standing around
67 minutes

Shots of the coach, crowd, cheerleaders, etc.
35 minutes

Commercials
63 minutes

2022, Daily Snark

Clocks in Sports

In addition to game clocks, many sports have play clocks and shot clocks. These clocks show a short amount of time. This is how long a player has to make a play or start an action.

Some sports also have timeouts. The length of a timeout varies by sport.

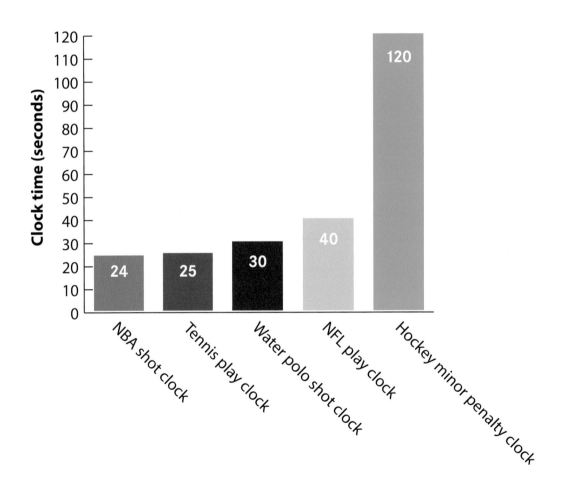

2022, NBA; 2012, Tennis.com; 2022, NCAA; 2022, NFL; 2022, Rookie Road

CHAPTER 2

Speed and Velocity

While the clock runs, athletes want to make the most of their time. They can accomplish a lot during the given time. They have to move, hit, and run as fast as possible.

Speed plays a huge role in sports. Speed is the rate of time at which an object or body moves along a path. Think of a runner. Their speed can be measured as they run around the track. From running to pitching to swimming, the faster the better.

Athletes' Average Speeds

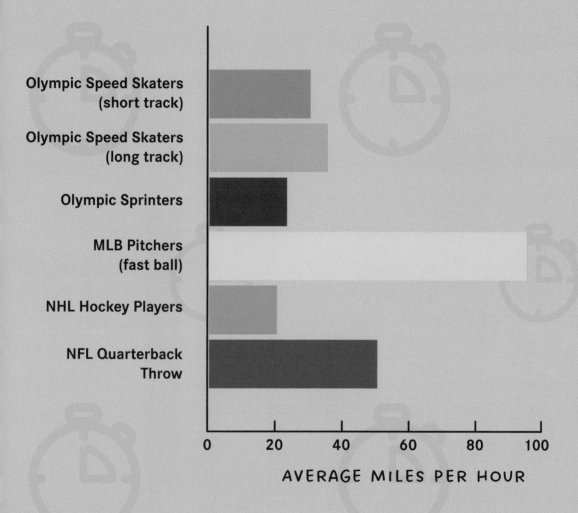

Olympic Speed Skaters (short track)

Olympic Speed Skaters (long track)

Olympic Sprinters

MLB Pitchers (fast ball)

NHL Hockey Players

NFL Quarterback Throw

AVERAGE MILES PER HOUR

0 20 40 60 80 100

2022, NBC Bay Area; 2021, New York Times; 2022, The Champlair.com; 2011, Wonderopolis.org; 2020, Reference.com

Athletes and coaches also track velocity. This is the rate and direction of an object's movement. Think of a baseball pitcher. The velocity of a pitch is the maximum speed of a pitch from its release until it crosses home plate. Right now, the MLB has more 100 miles (160 km) per hour pitches than any other time in its history.

Number of 100+ miles (160+ km) Per Hour Pitches

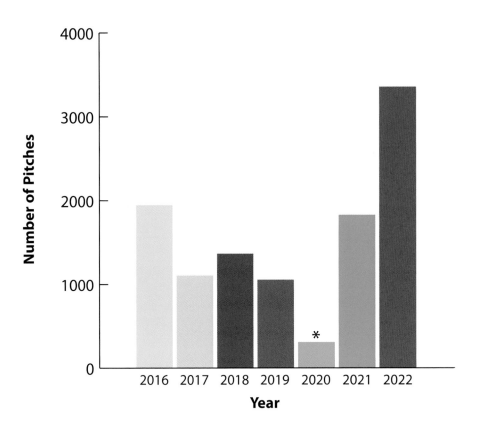

*The 2020 season was shortened because of the COVID-19 pandemic.

2022, MLB Statcast

Exit velocity is also measured in baseball. This is the speed with which the ball leaves a hitter's bat. The players with the most home runs and extra-base hits have high exit velocity. It's usually more than 90 miles (145 km) per hour. These players hit harder and farther.

Rank	Player	Team	Average Exit Velocity (mph)	Average Ball Distance (feet)	Average Home Run Distance (feet)
1	Judge, Aaron	New York Yankees	95.9	206	412
2	Alvarez, Yordan	Houston Astros	95.2	196	405
3	Trout, Mike	Los Angeles Angels	91.6	219	409
4	Schwarber, Kyle	Pittsburg Pirates	93.3	200	412
5	Stanton, Giancarlo	New York Yankees	95.0	163	402
6	Ohtani, Shohei	Los Angeles Angels	92.9	178	408
7	Riley, Austin	Atlanta Braves	92.5	183	411
8	Mountcastle, Ryan	Baltimore Orioles	91.3	188	407
9	Pederson, Joc	San Francisco Giants	93.2	192	407
10	Buxton, Byron	Minnesota Twins	92.9	194	410

2022, MLB; 2022, Baseball Savant

Average Speeds by Event

Sprinters run faster than long distance runners. A sprinter needs to keep up their pace for seconds. A long distance runner has to keep their pace for hours. These runners have a slower pace than sprinters. But they keep a steady pace for a much longer distance.

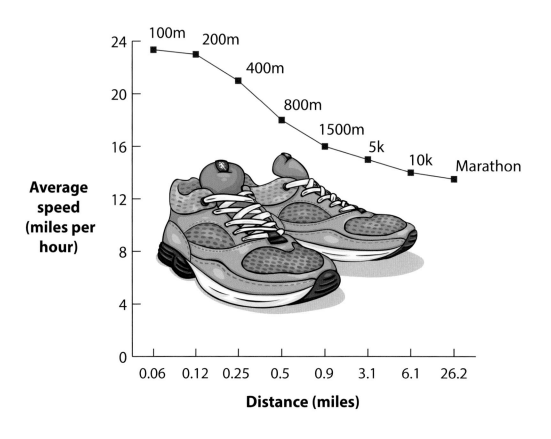

2021, New York Times

CHAPTER 3

Training for Victory

Athletes do whatever they can to perform their best. The fastest runner wins the race. The speed skater with the fastest time beats her opponents. The hockey player who can make the quickest shot is more likely to score. So athletes work hard to get faster. Players train harder. They need to be able to shave off time to win.

It may be seconds that matter during a game. But athletes put hours and hours into their training. Then they can make split-second decisions that can decide the outcome of a game.

An Athlete's Brain

System 1: Seconds to Act	System 2: Hours to Train
Fast	Slow
Unconscious	Conscious
Automatic	Effortful
Everyday Decisions	Complex Decisions
Error Prone	Reliable

2017, Ball State University Sports Link

System 1: Seconds to Act shows what an athlete's brain does in the moment. It is the thinking that is used during a game or performance.

System 2: Hours to Train puts in the hard, long hours. It shows what an athlete's brain does during their training.

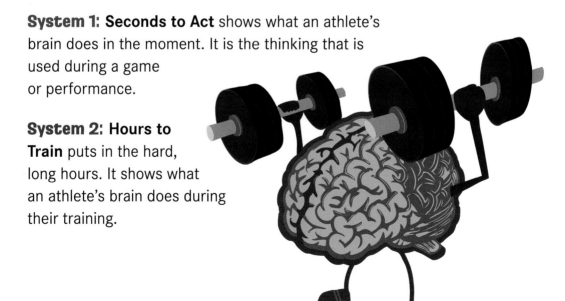

Coaches want the best chance of winning. This means they want to choose the best players for their teams. They need quarterbacks who can run quickly. They need wide receivers who are fast. A tenth of a second can make a difference in a player beating his opponent down the field.

Coaches look to the NFL Combine. There, they recruit players. The players run a 40-yard dash. These results help coaches assess the fastest players.

NFL Combine 2022

Player	Position	School	40-Yard Dash (seconds)
Kalon Barnes	CB	Baylor	4.23
Tariq Woolen	CB	Texas-San Antonio	4.26
Tyquan Thornton	WR	Baylor	4.28
Velus Jones Jr.	WR	Tennessee	4.31
Calvin Austin III	WR	Memphis	4.32
Zyon McCollum	CB	San Houston State (TX)	4.33
Danny Gray	WR	Southern Methodist (TX)	4.33
Nick Cross	SAF	Maryland	4.34
Bo Melton	WR	Rutgers	4.34
Christian Watson	WR	North Dakota State	4.36

2022, NFL

Altitude Affects Baseball

Training plays a big role in an athlete's performance. But there are other factors that a player cannot control. Elevation can play a role in how far a baseball travels.

FAST FACTS

- Land that is flat and close to the sea has a low elevation.
- At low elevations, the air is thick. There are high levels of air pressure. This pressure presses against moving objects. It slows them down.
- At high elevations, the air is thinner. There is less air pressure. Objects are not slowed down as much.

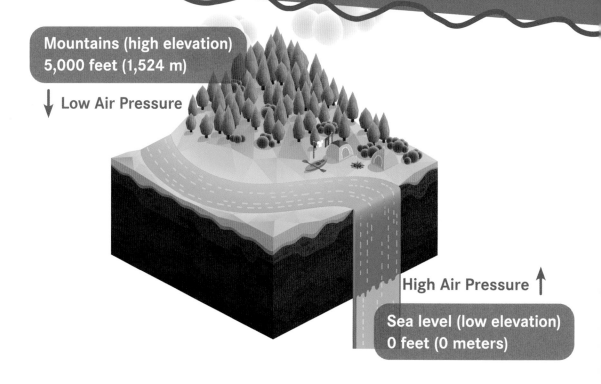

Mountains (high elevation)
5,000 feet (1,524 m)

↓ Low Air Pressure

High Air Pressure ↑

Sea level (low elevation)
0 feet (0 meters)

FAST FACTS

- The Seattle Mariners play by the sea. There, the elevation is 180 feet (55 m).
- With high air pressure, Mariners baseballs move slower.
- The Colorado Rockies play in the mountains. The elevation is 5,180 feet (1,579 m) above sea level.
- With low air pressure, Rockies baseballs move faster.

If the same ball was thrown at both parks, it would travel at different speeds.

SEATTLE MARINERS

A pitcher throws a fastball.

It travels at 100 miles (160 km) per hour.

It takes 0.413 seconds to reach the plate.

COLORADO ROCKIES

A pitcher throws the same fastball.

It travels at 102 miles (164 km) per hour.

It takes 0.405 seconds to reach the plate.

The Rockies ball travels 2 percent faster.

2021, CU Boulder Today; 2022, Maplogs; 2011, The Physics of Baseball; 2020, Baseball Cloud Blog

CHAPTER 4

Breaking Records

A game can come down to the last seconds. A lot can happen with only a few seconds left on the game clock.

Fractions of a second can break a world record time. It can come down to tenths or hundredths of a second! How fast is that? Think of it this way: The average human eye blinks in about a tenth of a second. So the short time it takes to blink could mean the difference between first and second place.

100-Meter Dash Times (Men)

Year	Time; Athlete	No.
1936	10.2 seconds; Jesse Owens	9
1956	10.1 seconds; Ira Murchinson	8
1968	9.95 seconds; Jim Hines	7
1972	9.9 seconds; Eddie Hart	6
1978	9.87 seconds; William Snoddy	5
1988	9.78 seconds; Carl Lewis	4
1996	9.69 seconds; Obadele Thompson	3
2008	9.68 seconds; Tyson Gay	2
2009	9.58 seconds; Usain Bolt	1

2021, World Athletics

Longest Games in MLB Playoff History

Some games are decided in the final seconds. Others take hours to decide the outcome. With extra innings or multiple overtimes, the length of the game can be longer than usual.

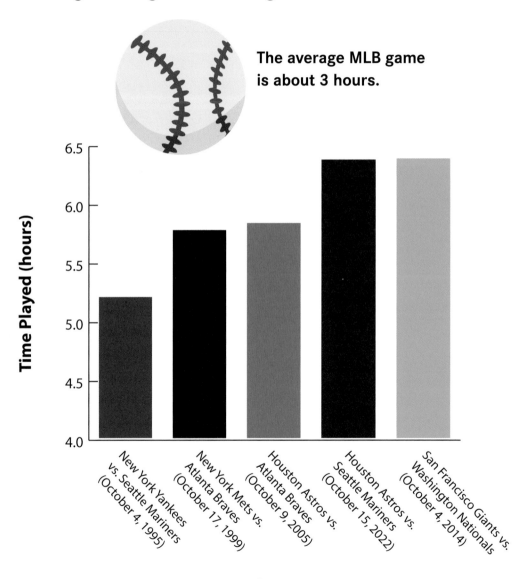

The average MLB game is about 3 hours.

Time Played (hours) / Game

- New York Yankees vs. Seattle Mariners (October 4, 1995)
- New York Mets vs. Atlanta Braves (October 17, 1999)
- Houston Astros vs. Atlanta Braves (October 9, 2005)
- Houston Astros vs. Seattle Mariners (October 15, 2022)
- San Francisco Giants vs. Washington Nationals (October 4, 2014)

2022, Sportsnaut

Longest Overtime Football Games

More than 90 percent of pro football games do not go into overtime.

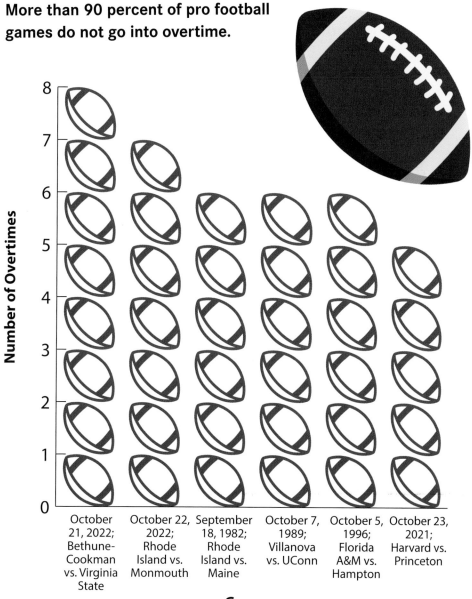

Number of Overtimes (y-axis): 0 – 8

Game (x-axis):
- October 21, 2022; Bethune-Cookman vs. Virginia State — 8
- October 22, 2022; Rhode Island vs. Monmouth — 7
- September 18, 1982; Rhode Island vs. Maine — 6
- October 7, 1989; Villanova vs. UConn — 6
- October 5, 1996; Florida A&M vs. Hampton — 6
- October 23, 2021; Harvard vs. Princeton — 5

2022, NCAA.com

Shortest Tennis Matches on Record

On average, a professional tennis match lasts anywhere from about 90 minutes to over 2 hours. But, some players have broken records by how quickly they were able to defeat their opponents.

Helen Wills defeated Joan Fry in 24 minutes. (1927)

Margaret Court defeated Darlene Hard in 24 minutes. (1963)

Jarkko Nieminen defeated Bernard Tomic in 28 minutes. (2014)

2021, Tennis Predict

Jack Harper defeated J. Sandiford in 18 minutes. (1946)

William Renshaw defeated John Hartley in 36 minutes. (1881)

Steffi Graf defeated Natasha Zvereva in 34 minutes. (1988)

Francisco Clavet defeated Jiang Shan in 25 minutes. (2001)

Activity

Time Yourself!

You know that athletes train to improve their skills and to increase their speed. Pick an activity that you want to improve. For example, you can time how long it takes you to run a mile or the time it takes to do 50 sit-ups.

Materials Needed:

- Stopwatch or timer
- Writing utensil
- Paper

Time yourself doing the same activity over the course of 5 days. Record your time each day on the table below. After 5 days, create a graph to show your results.

Day	Time
1	
2	
3	
4	
5	

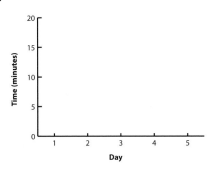

1. Did your time increase or decrease over the 5 days?

2. What did you do to improve your time?

3. Estimate the difference between your fastest time and your slowest time.

Learn More

Books

Buckley, James Jr. *It's a Numbers Game! Baseball: The Math Behind the Perfect Pitch, the Game-Winning Grand Slam, and So Much More!* Washington, DC: National Geographic Kids, 2021.

Storden, Thom. *Big-Time Football Records.* North Mankato, MN: Capstone Press, 2021.

Online Resources to Explore with an Adult

Kiddle. Tennis Facts for Kids

National Geographic Kids. 10 Facts About the Olympics!

Bibliography

NCAA.com. The Longest Overtime Games in FCS College Football History. October 2022.

New York Times. How Speed and Distance Dictate How Olympians Run. July 2021.

NFL.com. 2022 Combine Results. March 2022.

Sports Illustrated. How Long Is Soccer Halftime at the World Cup? November 2022.

World Athletics. Records by Event. February 2021.

Glossary

air pressure (AYR PREH-suhr) the weight of air molecules pressing down on objects

average (AH-ver-uhj) a number that is calculated by adding quantities together and then dividing by the total number of quantities

coverage (KUH-ver-uhj) the activity of reporting about an event on television

elevation (eh-luh-VAY-shun) the height of a place

exit velocity (EK-sut vuh-LAA-suh-tee) in baseball, the speed of the ball after it hits the bat

NFL Combine (N-F-L COM-bine) an annual event where coaches and scouts watch potential players complete physical and mental tests

opponents (uh-POH-nuhnts) people or teams who are competing against each other

outcome (OWT-kuhm) the result of an activity or process

play clocks (PLAY KLAHKS) clocks that count down how long teams or players have to make an action

professional (pruh-FEH-shuh-nuhl): having to do with a job that requires special skills, training, or experience

recruit (ruh-KROOT) to find the right people for the job or team

shave (SHAYV) to reduce something by taking away a small amount

shot clocks (SHOT KLAHKS) clocks that count down how long teams or players have to try to score

sprinters (SPRIN-turs) runners who race over a short distance at a very fast speed

stoppage (STAA-puhj) an occurrence in which play is stopped during a game

substitution (suhb-stuh-TOO-shun) the act of replacing one player for another

velocity (vuh-LAA-suh-tee) how quickly an object is moving

Index